NO HANDS ALLOWED
A Robbie Reader

Landon Donovan
World Class Soccer Star

Rebecca Thatcher Murcia

Mitchell Lane
PUBLISHERS

P.O. Box 196
Hockessin, Delaware 19707
Visit us on the web: www.mitchelllane.com
Comments? email us: mitchelllane@mitchelllane.com

A Robbie Reader
No Hands Allowed

Library of Congress Cataloging-in-Publication Data
Murcia, Rebecca Thatcher, 1962–
    Landon Donovan / by Rebecca Thatcher Murcia.
      p. cm. – (A Robbie reader. No hands allowed)
    Includes bibliographical references and index.
    ISBN 1-58415-386-5 (library bound)
    1. Donovan, Landon, 1982–Juvenile literature. 2. Soccer players–United States–
Biography–Juvenile literature. I. Title. II. Series.
GV942.7.D66M87 2005
796.334'092–dc22
                                                                          2004030740

ABOUT THE AUTHOR: Rebecca Thatcher Murcia grew up in Garrison, New York, and graduated from the University of Massachusetts at Amherst. She was a daily newspaper reporter–mostly in Texas–for 14 years. She is a soccer coach and player in Akron, Pennsylvania, where she lives with her husband and two sons. She is the author of other soccer biographies for Mitchell Lane Publishers, including *David Beckham* and *Freddy Adu.*

PHOTO CREDITS: Cover, p. 8–Eliot J. Schechter/Getty Images; pp. 1, 3–Brian Bahr/ Allsport;p. 4–Pascal Guyot/AFP/Getty Images; p. 6–(top) Greg Wood/AFP/Getty Images; p. 6 (bottom)–Shaun Botterill/Getty Images; p. 10–Martin Bureau/AFP/Getty Images; pp. 12, 21–Jeff Gross/Getty Images; p. 14–Eliot J. Schechter/AFP/Getty Images; pp. 16, 20–Stephen Dunn/Getty Images; p. 18 (top photo)–Brad Balonick/SSP/Time Life Pictures/Getty Images; p. 18 (bottom photo)–Michael Stahlschmidt/SSP/Time Life Pictures/Getty Images; p. 22–Ronald Martinez/Getty Images; p. 24–Yuri Cortez/AFP/ Getty Images; p. 26–Doug Benc/Getty Images; p. 27–STR/AFP/Getty Images; p. 28– Alex Livesey/Getty Images.

ACKNOWLEDGMENTS: The following story has been thoroughly researched, and to the best of our knowledge, represents a true story. While every possible effort has been made to ensure accuracy, the publisher will not assume liability for damages caused by inaccuracies in the data, and makes no warranty on the accuracy of the information contained herein. This story has not been authorized nor endorsed by Landon Donovan nor anyone associated with Landon Donovan.

TABLE OF CONTENTS

This is Landon Donovan playing for the United States in the 2002 World Cup. Donovan is one of the bright young stars of American soccer.

Donovan Shines

Landon Donovan was playing for the United States in a very important soccer game. His team was playing against Mexico in the **World Cup championship.**

Mexico's team had been winning most of its games. The United States had also done well, winning against Portugal and earning a tie with South Korea. The game against Mexico was important, because if the United States lost, they would be out of the **tournament.** Both teams were playing hard. The United States was winning with one goal. Mexico had not scored.

Eddie Lewis, one of the American players, escaped a Mexican player with the ball and ran down the side of the field. Landon Donovan ran

5

Landon Donovan used his speed to run into the pages of U.S. soccer history when he scored this header against Mexico at the 2002 World Cup.

A Mexican defender shows his disappointment as Landon Donovan celebrates his goal against Mexico.

down the middle of the field. A Mexican defender ran with Donovan, but he could not run as fast as Donovan. Lewis kicked the ball into the air, right to the space in front of Donovan. Donovan leaped into the air and hit the ball hard with his forehead. It flew past the Mexican goalkeeper and into the net.

It was a big goal. It helped the United States win against Mexico and advance to the quarterfinals of the 2002 World Cup. That was the best the United States had done in the World Cup in 72 years.

People were thrilled to see Donovan, who was only 20 years old, play so well. But that was not new. He had been amazing crowds since he was a boy.

7

Landon Donovan, shown here in his San Jose Earthquakes uniform, was the first American teenager to sign with a top-level professional club in Europe.

A California Childhood

Landon Timothy Donovan was born on March 4, 1982, in Ontario, California. He grew up in Redlands, California, which is west of Los Angeles. Landon's mother, Donna, was a teacher. His father, Tim Donovan, was a former **semiprofessional** hockey player. Landon has an older brother, Joshua, and a twin sister, Tristan.

When Landon was nine months old, he began walking. That is about three months earlier than when most babies begin walking. Soon after Landon could walk, he began to run and play soccer with Joshua.

Landon's father left the family when Landon was about two years old. His mother had to raise her three children by herself. She

Landon Donovan gets ready to fight for the ball during a game against Cameroon in 2003. Donovan brings speed, power, and a good sense of teamwork to the U.S. national team.

worked hard, but the family did not have a lot of money.

Landon's mother knew her son was good at soccer when he was five years old and in kindergarten. She signed him up to play on a team of six- and seven-year-olds. Landon scored seven goals in his first game. From that moment on, he always wanted to play soccer.

His mother made sure Landon did his homework. She also let him learn how to play the violin. But soccer was always very important to him. "I just loved it," he said. "I didn't like anything else."

Landon Donovan always plays to win. Here he kisses the Alan I. Rothenberg trophy after the San Jose Earthquakes defeat the Chicago Fire 4-2 in the MLS Cup in November 2003 at the Home Depot Center in Carson, California.

A Teenage Star

Soccer coaches noticed how well Landon played. If his mother did not have money for soccer, they told her that Landon could still play.

When Landon was 16 years old, the U.S. men's soccer team played in the 1998 World Cup in France. Landon would go to school early during the World Cup so that he could watch the games on television before his classes started. He would also ask the teachers to let the class watch the World Cup during school, but they usually said no. The U.S. men lost all their games and finished the tournament in last place. It was a big disappointment for American soccer fans.

Here Landon Donovan (back) is trying to get the ball away from Diego of Brazil. With Landon Donovan on the U.S. national team, the United States was able to defeat Mexico at the 2002 World Cup. But top teams such as Brazil and Argentina are still difficult for the United States national team. Brazil won this Gold Cup game in 2003.

Landon was picked for the Under-17 **national** (NAH-shuh-nul) team. With his skill at scoring goals, the team did very well. They won fourth place at the Under-17 World Championship in New Zealand. Landon was given the most valuable player award. His best game was against New Zealand, in which he scored the game-winning point.

Landon had two other great games with the U.S. Under-17 team. They beat Argentina (ARE-jen-TEEN-a) 4-3, with Landon scoring two goals. They also defeated the Tampa Bay Mutiny, a **professional** (pro-FEH-shuh-nul) team, 2-0, with Landon scoring both goals.

Coaches from the best professional teams in Europe noticed.

15

In 2003, Landon Donovan led the San Jose Earthquakes to the Major League Soccer championship, scoring two goals in the 4-2 win over Chicago Fire. Here he holds a trophy during the MLS Gala Awards Ceremony at the Kodak Theatre on November 22, 2003.

To Germany and Back

Landon was more than just a soccer star. With his high forehead, dark eyebrows, and curly black hair, many people thought he was handsome. When he scored a goal, he would often do something a little crazy. He was becoming known as one of the best young American players—and a very interesting person.

Bayer Leverkusen in Germany is one of the best soccer clubs in Europe. Coaches from Bayer Leverkusen offered Landon a four-year **contract** in which he would be paid $100,000 a year. Landon's mother wanted him to stay in the United States and go to college, but Tim Donovan urged him to go. Landon, who was

At the 2002 World Cup, the United States lost to Germany 1-0 in the quarter-finals. The game was very close, however, and Landon Donovan played very well. Here, he reacts after a German defender used his hand to keep the ball out of his goal.

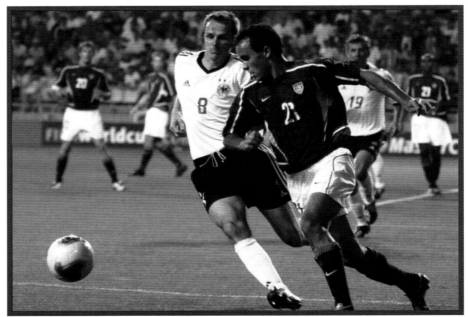

Early in the match, Donovan passed the ball between the legs of one German defender, and then dribbled by another. He shot hard and Germany's goalkeeper, Oliver Kahn, made a big save.

just turning 17, was not sure what to do. "I was just a kid, wanting to have fun," he said later.

He decided to play for Bayer in Germany. He was the first American teenager to get a contract with a top-level European club.

The change did not go very well. Landon practiced hard, but he did not play in very many games. He did not like the cold, cloudy weather. He missed his family, especially his sister, Tristan.

Landon kept working hard at soccer. He could have stayed in Germany and earned more than $1 million a year, but he decided to come back to the United States. He would play for the San Jose (hoe-ZAY) Earthquakes in California. Instead of over $1 million in Germany, he would earn about $350,000. This was unusual. Many sports stars want to earn as much money as possible. Landon wanted to come home more than he wanted to be rich.

When he first joined the Earthquakes, he did not score very many goals. He was also busy playing for the U.S. men's national team. He played in the 1999 Olympics, and he helped the team qualify for the 2002 World Cup.

Landon Donovan celebrates with the fans after his team, the San Jose Earthquakes, win against the Los Angeles Galaxy in 2003.

Landon Donovan keeps the ball, and keeps defenders guessing, with his excellent control and smooth dribbling. Here he is playing for the San Jose Earthquakes against Chicago Fire at the Major League Soccer championships.

Landon Donovan played for the United States against Mexico in what is known as a friendly, or exhibition game at the Cotton Bowl in Dallas in 2004. Donovan played well and had two excellent chances to score, but the United States won 1-0 on a goal by Eddie Pope.

A Star at Home

After the U.S. players won against Mexico at the 2002 World Cup, they had to play against Germany. Germany's soccer team was very good. The captain, Oliver Kahn, was one of the best goalkeepers in the world. The Americans played well. They passed well. Donovan had some good shots. Kahn stopped them all.

The Americans were defeated, but they had done very well. Donovan had scored against Mexico and against Portugal. He came home to a hero's welcome. He was on the cover of *Sports Illustrated* and appeared on television shows such as *Late Night with David Letterman*.

People began showing up at the Earthquakes' games. They shouted, "Landon! Landon!" And Donovan just kept getting better.

In 2003 he led the San Jose Earthquakes to the national championship. He scored two goals in the 4-2 victory over the Chicago Fire. In 2004, the coach of the men's national team, Bruce Arena, made Donovan captain of the team. "He's a fantastic player," Arena said. Donovan's national team jersey number is 21.

With Donovan as captain, the United States beat Panama 6-0. They also won against El Salvador, 2-0. In early 2005, the United States defeated Trinidad and Tobago 2-1 in the first game of the final round of 10 World Cup qualifying games.

Donovan returned to Germany to play for Bayer Leverkusen in January 2005. He wanted to fulfill the contract he had signed as a teenager. As an international soccer standout, he was sure his second try at playing soccer in Europe would go better than his first. But it didn't. Donovan did not get much playing time in Germany. In April 2005, Donovan announced he would return to play in the United States for the Los Angeles Galaxy.

Donovan is a star, but he is still young. If American soccer fans are lucky, he will continue to thrill crowds with his skill and speed for many more years.

U.S. coach Bruce Arena made Landon Donovan the captain of the U.S. national team in the fall of 2004, after Claudio Reyna was injured. Here, Donovan wears the captain's armband against El Salvador. The United States won 2-0.

Landon Donovan played hard in the semi-finals of the the Major League Soccer Western Conference in 2004. But San Jose was eliminated after winning the first game 2-0 and losing the second game 0-3.

Landon Donovan continued to be the captain of the United States national team in World Cup qualifying in 2005. Here he is shown playing against Trinidad and Tobago. The United States won 2-1.

Landon Donovan of Bayer Leverkusen plays hard during the UEFA Champions League first match at Anvil in Liverpool, England, on February 22, 2005, but Bayer lost 3-1.

1982 Born on March 4 in Ontario, California

1997 Joins U.S. Youth Soccer's Olympic Development Program

1998 Plays for the U.S. Under-17 national team

1999 Goes to Germany to play for Bayer Leverkusen

2000 Plays for the U.S. senior men's national team for the first time

2001 Joins the San Jose Earthquakes in California

2002 Helps the U.S. men's team reach the quarterfinals of the World Cup

2003 Scores twice in the San Jose Earthquakes championship game against the Chicago Fire

2004 Captains the U.S. men's team in World Cup qualifying games

2005 Returns to Bayer Leverkusen; then comes back to play in the U.S. in April

championship (CHAM-pee-un-ship)—an event at which a winner is declared the best of all the contenders.

contract (KAHN-trakt)—a written agreement in which one person or company agrees to provide a service or product to another person or company.

national (NA-shuh-nul)—having to do with an entire country.

professional (pro-FEH-shuh-nul)—a person who is paid to perform.

semiprofessional (SEM-ee pro-FEH-shuh-nul)—a person who is paid to perform on a part-time basis.

tournament (TUR-na-ment)—a series of games that leads to a championship.

World Cup (WERLD kup)—the international tournament for outdoor soccer.

Magazine Articles

Friedman, Nick. "Happy Landon!" *Sports Illustrated for Kids,* September 2001.

Hernandez, Dylan. "Pitch Perfect." *Sports Illustrated for Kids,* August 2004.

_____. "Striking It Big." *Sports Illustrated for Kids,* June 2003.

Web Addresses

JockBio.com: "Landon Donovan"
www.jockbio.com/Bios/Donovan_Landon/ Donovan_bio.html

Major League Soccer
www.mlsnet.com

U.S. Soccer Federation
www.ussoccer.com

Bayer Leverkusen
www.bayer04.de

Works Consulted

Davidson, Gary. "Donovan Sets Sights High as Budding Star of American Program." *Soccer Times,* March 9, 1999.

"Happy Ending Still Possible for Young Soccer Star." *San Jose Mercury News,* May 7, 2001.

"Soccer's Rock Star: Quakes' Donovan." *Contra Costa Times,* July 30, 2002.

Team USA: Coming of Age. (DVD) Reedswain, Inc., 2002.

INDEX

32